Bedworth
Past & Present

JOHN BURTON

SUTTON PUBLISHING

Sutton Publishing Limited
Phoenix Mill · Thrupp · Stroud
Gloucestershire · GL5 2BU

First published 2002

Title page: Bedworth from the south-west, 1998. The aerial photograph shows the size of the cemetery, the large number of flat roofs on modern buildings, and the impact that the late Victorian Park Road (running along the bottom of the picture) had on the edge of Bedworth. The Miners' Welfare Park is on the right, and Nicholas Chamberlaine School, with its huge playing fields, is top right. (*Nuneaton & Bedworth Borough Council*)

British Library Cataloguing in Publication Data
A catalogue record for this book is available from the British Library.

ISBN 0-7509-2801-8

Typeset in 10.5/13.5 Photina.
Typesetting and origination by Sutton Publishing Limited.
Printed and bound in England by J.H. Haynes & Co. Ltd, Sparkford.

> *For Madge Harrison, who, at ninety-three,*
> *still speaks with more eloquence and wisdom about old Bedworth*
> *than anyone else I have met.*

Aerial view of Bedworth, *c.* 1965, showing the town at a pivotal time of change. Coventry Road becomes High Street at the top end of the cemetery. Rye Piece Ringway has not yet been built, but on the far right, half way up the picture, is the Zion Baptist chapel. Most of Spitalfields to the right of High Street has been cleared, except for the buildings fronting the road. The Tower House has gone – demolished in 1963. Church Street has gone, but the line of the road can be seen. The buildings just to the north of the church were about to come down to make way for the rectangular All Saints Square.

CONTENTS

INTRODUCTION

It has often been noted how rapidly our landscape has changed since the last war, particularly the centres of many of our towns and cities that were devastated during the 1960s and 1970s. Postwar austerity gave way, in the 1960s, to a time of increased prosperity and confidence that expressed itself in a desire to rebuild our towns and cities. Huge areas of land were given up to the all-pervading motor car. Road builders were as insensitive to human scale as the railway pioneers had been a century earlier.

Bedworth was no exception to these changes. During the 1960s the writer Ian Nairn cast his perceptive eye over what was happening in Britain. He wrote acerbic and witty pieces about architecture for the *Observer*, as well as being a natural television performer. He is sadly missed. A story goes that he was invited to Bedworth by the then Urban District Council, wined and dined, and asked for his advice about redeveloping the town centre. His advice was to do nothing, and to retain the charm and eccentricity of old Bedworth. Within a decade the entire town centre had gone, the curves and slopes banished, to be replaced by All Saints Square and Congreve Walk!

Change is inevitable, of course, but in many places babies were sluiced away with the bath water, and now towns are trying to re-establish individuality and distinctiveness, often employing town centre managers to help in the task. We do not know what the original 1715 almshouses looked like in Bedworth, but we can be pretty certain that they were less attractive and less impressive than the 1840 replacements which we now admire. The old Bedworth UDC was responsible for the awful Kings House, a building ideally suited to Coventry, or any big city, but totally out of scale in a town the size of Bedworth. Yet the same authority was responsible for the Civic Hall, a clear improvement on the ramshackle and run-down area known as Spitalfields.

This book shows readers what Bedworth looked like before 1970. For young people and newcomers to the town it will be a revelation. To those who remember the old town the following pages will bring a feeling of nostalgia for what has been lost. The new pictures, mostly taken during the summer of 2001, show the often startling changes which have taken place, and help to place the old pictures in an understandable context. It attempts to be a completely new book and only a couple of dozen or so photographs appeared in the earlier, and now out of print *Bedworth in Old Photographs* (Sutton, 1988, rp. 1992).

I am enormously grateful to all those who have let me use their collections over the years, and particularly in the last two years to those who have lent pictures to The Parsonage Project Bedworth's Heritage Centre, many of which I have been allowed to copy. My photographing of Bedworth over the last thirty years is a token of thanks to those whose generosity with earlier pictures make books like this possible. Where I can remember them I have credited owners after each photograph.

There is a strong interest in local history in Bedworth that will surely continue. However between the publication of my two books we have lost two stalwart local experts, both personal friends and fellow enthusiasts. I pay tribute to Gay Parker and Fred Phillips for their unstinting support and interest in so many aspects of local studies. We miss them still, but their work lives on.

1

Nicholas Chamberlaine Almshouses

The landscaping in front of the almshouses was an inspired piece of cooperation between Nuneaton and Bedworth Borough Council and the trustees of the almshouses, for it swept away the railings and wall and brought the old Market Place, now renamed All Saints Square, into real contact with the almshouses. The water feature is a delight. The conifers planted in the mid-1970s had become too large, so in 2000 the area was replanted. This photograph was taken from the top of the shops opposite in 1990. At the time Joe Davis ran a sports shop there, and I am grateful to him for allowing me to scramble over his roof.

Female residents, or inmates as they were then called, of the almshouses, 1911. This picture and the one below were taken possibly to celebrate George V's accession, but certainly to adorn the pages of a self-congratulatory booklet by William Johnson MP, entitled *My Native Bedworth*. They look an unhappy bunch of ladies, in need of teeth, but they had no doubt endured hard times in Victorian Bedworth. Back row, left to right: Harriet Moore, 58; Eliza Richards, 68; Harriet Critchlow, 73; Sarah Smith, 74; Harriet Jephcote, 64; Jane Emma Ford, 60; Henretta Haywood, 68; Sarah Hammersley, 73; Leah Moore, 65. Front row: Ann Walker, 72; Eliza Tibbets, 68; Eliza Moore, 85; Sarah Lucas, 68; Ann Wilkinson, 73; Annie Camwell, 71; Naomi Jaques, 69; Emma Hall, 74.

Male inmates, 1911. They look slightly happier than the ladies, and like them, they are wearing the uniform that was provided for them and had to be worn. Outworn uniform was replaced during Whit week, and some of the women's wear was made by girls at the Central School. Back row, left to right: Elijah Hall, 68; Richard Rally, 69; William Hunt, 83; Thomas Harvey, 65; Henry Deeming, 72; Harry Tedds, 69. Front row: Enoch Harrison, 71; William Johnson, 72; William Richards, 62; Edward Mills, 76; George Wagstaffe, 72; William Lydster, 73.

Almshouse residents in the 1920s. There are some wonderful expressions on the faces of these people. A relative of Eileen Baker is on the back row, and two of the faces were used as models for Abe and Ada in The Parsonage Project (see page 128). (*Eileen Baker Collection*)

Millennium portrait of most of the residents in July 2000, sitting just to the left of the door in the pictures opposite. Back rows, left to right: Sheila Whitehead (warden), Paul Whitehead, Rene Twigger, Bill Twigger, Ida Trivitt, Edgar Carter, Joan Corcoran, John Kersly, Jan Paling, Floss Fletcher, Rene Garnier, Vera Pettifer, Chick Farmer, Betty Hewitt, Betty Rollaston, Annie Pickard, Dot Vaughan, Grace Whitehead, Glynn Vaughan. Seated: Marjorie Sylvester, Edith Smith, Pat Bosworth, Betty Farmer, Dolly Kean, Joe Pickard.

Since they were built in 1840 the almshouses have been used as a meeting place for celebrations like Whit Walks and Sunday school anniversaries, coronations and festivities, and they appear as a background in countless photographs. It was no surprise then that the mayor for 2001–2, Councillor Bill Hancox, and his wife, Councillor Sheila Hancox, both representing local wards, chose the almshouses as a background for some of their official photographs.

The quadrangle, shown here with the flower beds and hanging baskets at their best in August 2001, is a lovely foreground to the early Victorian gothic buildings, designed to look Elizabethan, and still home for some thirty residents who are proud to be part of a tradition stretching back to 1715. The small building with stone roof is the pumphouse and the section of the building beneath the clock tower is the Governors' Hall.

2

All Saints Square (the old Market Place)

This is one of the classic views of old Bedworth, showing market day in the mid-1920s. There was a slight bend in the road behind the photographer and Market Place became Market Street. To the bottom left, where the couple are standing, is Church Street which curved round towards the north door of the parish church. Beyond Fletcher the butcher, at no. 17, is the lodge to the almshouses where the warden lived. It was pulled down in about 1970 and the Christmas tree and Boots the chemist stand in its place. This postcard view was taken from an upper room in the Newdegate Arms public house (see page 29).

CHAMBERLAIN HOUSE
BEDWORTH

Mr *opposite Chamberlain's Charity*
Lovell

Bo! of John Gibberd,
& Woollen Draper.
ER, HOSIER & HABERDASHER.
Family Mourning. — Funerals Furnished.
Bonnets, Ribbons, Flowers, Lace, Gloves &c.
GROCER & TEA DEALER.

1861
January

This bill heading survived against all the odds. It was bricked up in an old range in a building on the corner of Market Place and Mill Street; many items emerged scorched and charred. The bill is from John Gibberd in 1861. Its interest is the attention given by Gibberd to the shop's position, 'opposite Chamberlain's Charity', which seems to have been more important than its position in the Market Place. He even calls the building Chamberlain House. This is one of several variant spellings of Chamberlaine. (*Owen Buckler Collection*)

The Gibberd family were long-established retailers with shops in Longford and Leamington. They are still in Coventry, but in 1901 they sold the Bedworth premises to J.C. Smith of Stratford. Smith's was to become part of the tradition of Bedworth, offering value for money over a huge range of goods. They stayed in business (though by then owned by Debenhams) until the redevelopment of this part of town in the very early 1970s. This picture shows the store in the early 1920s.

The postcard above dates from 1907. Smith's can be seen on the left. The company was later to take over most of the buildings in the row. The little shop beyond the milk delivery cart was owned by Mr Mole who sold the original postcard. The chain railings stood in front of the almshouse wall until the First World War. The picture below was taken from the same spot in August 2001.

Shopfronts change very often now, but even before the war there were changes of ownership. On the left of the postcard above is Mason the grocer. Earlier photographs show it as Edmand's, and it may be that earlier still it was Darlison's (see page 30). Later it was owned by Bunney's (see page 23). Next door was the Maypole, but that too changed hands in later years as the Maypole moved up the Market Place to the other side of Smith's. The picture below was taken in August 2001 from almost exactly the same spot.

Smiths & Sons were at their most successful between the wars, and advertisements like this one appeared everywhere. The tailoring department, shown below in the 1950s, was visible from the passageway down the side of the store. There is still a huge folk memory of Smith's in Bedworth, both among people who worked there and those who fondly recall purchasing clothes or furniture.

For nearly a century images were collected for the Warwickshire Photographic Survey. Bedworth was covered by F.C. Harpur in 1948. He produced some thirty images, ten of which appear in this book. They add a wonderful quality, because they allow us to see most of the town as it appeared in those postwar years. The picture above was taken outside the almshouses, where the no. 20 Coventry bus stopped. (*Birmingham Central Library*)

The same spot in September 2001; the changes are startling.

Both these views look towards the Market Place/All Saints Square from the bottom of Leicester Street. Above is one of Harpur's 1948 images, with Smith's in the distance. The Bass Burton Ales sign is outside the Hit or Miss (see page 42). The military uniform is a clue that the picture was taken close to wartime. (*Birmingham Central Library*)

The picture above was taken in September 2001. The shop line was pushed back during the 1970s redevelopment of Leicester Street. The tall chimneys belong to the parsonage, part of the almshouses. In this shot I moved slightly to the left to include the Collycroft Beer Festival and Lottery signs, which help to 'place' the picture for future reference.

A line of shops in Market Place, *c*. 1900. At that time it was a mixture of private homes and shops, and the shopkeepers generally lived above the shop. These were opposite the almshouse wall and railings. (*Magson Collection*)

The same spot in September 2001.

John Magson started his business in 1884. Here he is outside the outfitter's shop. Other members of the family joined the business. The picture below shows that the Magsons expanded into the meat business in the 1920s and 1930s. They were also builders (see page 114) and dabbled in bicycles in 1900. (*Magson Collection*)

Melias, *c.* 1920. This grocer's occupied two properties over the years. The picture above shows their first shop on the left-hand end of the line (see page 16), when butter was 1*s* a pound, and the windows were packed with goods. Later they moved two doors away, and the picture opposite shows the shop in the 1930s. (*Jean Thompson Collection*)

Left is the same line with its modern shops, September 2001.

Small shops often employed a lot of people. Melias had ten staff when this picture was taken in the 1930s. The manager was Mr Smith and the manageress was Miss Nash. (*Jean Thompson Collection*)

Melias, shown above, stood where Shipley's Amusements now is. In the 1930s neither travel shops nor amusement arcades existed in Bedworth; now they have prime sites. In the 1930s floral decoration would have been an affectation; now the town centre is full of hanging baskets and canopy displays.

Bedworth Market, probably 1890s. This is the earliest picture of the market I have seen. It shows an open market with traders laying out their goods in the road and on boxes. (*Magson Collection*)

Sixty years later this picture was taken from the same spot, but looking the other way. By the 1950s there were stalls and canopies for traders, as this view shows. (*Ronald Edmands Collection*)

When the Market Place was rebuilt and the road closed to vehicles the market was moved to its present site off Mill Street. It remained for twenty-five years until, in 1996, it was rebuilt on the same site, but with a roof and lighting. During the rebuilding the market returned to its old home in All Saints Square. The picture above shows crowded stalls on either side of the raised flower beds.

This stall is in the new market hall. It was part of a first for the town when, in July 2001, the local Rotary club organised a Sunday craft market that was very successful, and reflected the hard work of Ken Elliott and his team. Selling assorted cuddly toys on this stall were Gwen Earp, Jan Hill and Maureen Earp.

Market Street, 1948. The road changed from Market Place to Market Street at the junction with Church Street (about where Woolworths is now). The building on the right is the Newdegate Arms, one of many pubs in a mining town. On the left are the ironmonger Parson, Sherwin, Skeltons the chemist and Boots. The three-wheel delivery vehicle belonged to the LMS and had come from the railway station. (*Birmingham Central Library*)

The same spot in August 2001.

This shop appears elsewhere as Edmands and later as Masons. It was one of several sites occupied by Bunney's. On the left a new building is being constructed. When it was completed Bunney's moved into it, and the old building was demolished to make way for Congreve Walk, which more or less followed the same route as the yard on the right. The building on the right is the side of J.C. Smith. (*Ted Veasey Collection*)

The picture above was taken as Bunney's were about to close down at the end of the 1980s.

HENRY BUNNEY,

HAIR DRESSER AND PERFUMER,

OPPOSITE THE CHURCH, BEDWORTH,

DEALER IN EVERY DESCRIPTION OF

TOYS AND FANCY GOODS,

Musical Instruments, Writing Desks,

WORK BOXES, COMBS, BRUSHES, JEWELLERY,

GERMAN SILVER & METAL SPOONS, CUTLERY, FISHING TACKLE,

FANCY BASKETS, STATIONERY, ETC.

N.B.—BIRD STUFFER and PRESERVER of ANIMALS, to imitate nature in all its perfection, **ON THE MOST REASONABLE TERMS.**

YOU WILL ALWAYS FIND

The Best Variety, The Newest Styles, and the Lowest Prices, at

BUNNEY'S CHEAP SHOP

MARKET PLACE, BEDWORTH.

Noted for every kind of Useful, Ornamental, Fancy and Domestic Articles; French, German, and other Goods suitable for presents, in wood, bone, Gilt, Ivory, Pearl, Tortoiseshell, &c. &c.

JEWELLERY.

Gold, Silver, and Plated Brooches, Lockets, Chains, Guards, Earrings, Studs &c. SOLID GOLD WEDDING RINGS from 7s. GERMAN, SWISS, and AMERICAN CLOCKS and WATCHES.

STATIONERY.

Note Paper 5 Quires for 8½d. Envelopes 4d. per 100. Day, Cash, Memorandum and Pocket Books, Bibles, Prayers, Church Services, Poetry, Verse and Birthday Cards, &c. &c.

CUTLERY.

Pen and Pocket Knives, Table Knives, from 2s. 6d. half dozen. Nickel Silver Tea Spoons from 1s. half dozen; Scissors from 4d. per Pair; Tea Caddies, Trays, Waiters, Work Boxes, Candle Sticks, Brushes, Brooms, and Hardware generally.

Iron Bedsteads, Full Size, from 12s. 9d.

HOSIERY & HABERDASHERY

Goods in every style Collars, Cuffs, Socks, Stockings, Velvets, braids, Trimmings, Binding, Buttons, Belts, Braces, Elastic Webs, Cotton, Tapes, and Smallware Generally. AN IMMENSE ASSORTMENT OF

BOOTS & SHOES.

Particular attention is given to this branch of business and we can warrant them well made, one trial will convince that at least 40 per cent may be saved by purchasing as above.

WOMENS ELASTIC SIDES.						MEN'S ELASTIC SIDES.						
2/11	3/6	4/	4/6	5/	5/6	7/6	8/6	9/	10/	11/1	12/3	14/6

The Bunney family came to Bedworth in the seventeenth century, and they have made enormous contributions to the town ever since. Their name appears in connection with mining, brick making, building, and non-conformism. They have traded as general shopkeepers, specialist decorators, and even briefly as photographers. The advertisement above is out of sequence, but is placed here for the family connection, and indeed the shop was only a few yards away. Henry offered an odd mixture of services in 1870, from hairdressing to musical instruments and bird stuffing on the most reasonable terms – an important consideration for poverty-stricken Bedworth!

This delightful advertisement from before the First World War talks of Bunney's Cheap Shop, not a phrase we would use today. We prefer more anodyne phrases like Best Value, or Lowest Prices. Then you could set up home for £5, or buy a bed and a wedding ring for £1.

Market Street, 1948. The railway delivery vehicle seen on page 22 is still here. Beyond it are Barclays Bank and Pearks the grocer. On the left is Worthington's grocery shop, and beyond it the Bedworth & Foleshill News office. J.C. Smith's is in the distance. (*Birmingham Central Library*)

This superb photograph is of the staff at Worthington's about twenty years after the top picture was taken. The ladies are Lily Bettam, Gladys Haywood (the wife of Bill Haywood, the manager), Olwyn Randle (now Morris) and Doris Mortiboys.

NEURALGIA, OR A SHILLING?

WHICH?

Do you prefer to suffer from Neuralgia rather than pay a Shilling for a Remedy that will give you almost immediate Relief? Lester's Sovereign Remedy has cured too many and too wide a variety of cases of Neuralgia to leave any doubt of its wonderful curative power. It is speedy, sure, and safe. Could not possibly harm anyone, but never fails to give quick Relief from any form of Tic or Neuralgia.

WORTH A SOVEREIGN; COSTS A SHILLING.

W. H. LESTER,

DISPENSING CHEMIST,

Market St., BEDWORTH.

W.H. Lester had a chemist's shop in Market Street, and there were two others within yards. Before the NHS there was a huge demand for inexpensive medicines, many of which offered unrealistic remedies for minimum outlay. The Victorian era was a great period for quack medicine, but both Lester's and Oates's claimed to be able to cure neuralgia for 1s. The Oates advertisement dates from about 1900, the Lester one from a few years later. Lester also had branches in Nuneaton.

NEURALGIA! NEURALGIA! NEURALGIA!

There is no need to go on suffering the excruciating pain caused by

Tic, Face-Ache, and Neuralgia,

When a complete cure is at hand.

Rheumatic Pains may also be relieved by

Oates' Celebrated Neuralgia Mixture.

" In the most acute cases this Marvellous Remedy never fails to give relief."

This is the Testimony of hundreds who have taken this wonderful Medicine.

Secure a bottle to-day—It may be worth its weight in gold to-morrow.

PRICE, 1/- PER BOTTLE.

Prepared by

C. H. OATES, M.P.S., Dispensing Chemist,

BEDWORTH

The interior of Oates the chemist, 1900. Through marriage the shop changed its name to Skelton. When the town was redeveloped in the 1970s the shop moved to Congreve Walk. It is still there and still called Skelton's, though the family no longer own it. The interior of that shop is shown below in September 2001.

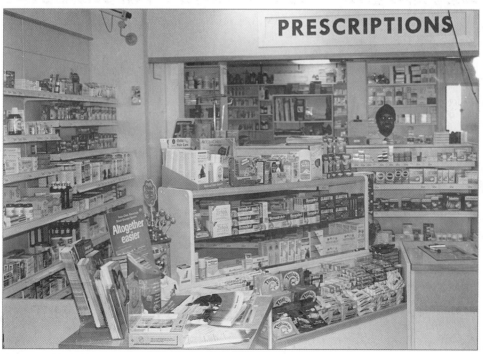

The pictures at the top of this page and page 29 were taken on the same day, *c.* 1914. The one above shows the corner of Church Street (bottom left, where the cobbles are). That street no longer exists; part of Woolworths and the adjacent Supercigs were built over it. Across the top is the old White Swan, and down the right-hand side the almshouse wall and lodge. The chimney in the distance belonged to Pickering's hat factory. Tesco is now on the site. The picture below was taken in September 2001 from the same spot.

The photographer walked 20 yards and turned his camera round to look up Market Street. There are two adjacent pubs, the Newdegate Arms and The Bull's Head; the buildings stand in front of the parish church. Had the planners been less keen on straight lines in the redevelopment of Bedworth it might have been possible to allow the whole church to be seen from All Saints Square. The picture below was taken from the same spot in September 2001.

The Darlison family is recorded as having shops in High Street, Market Street and Mill Street at various times during the nineteenth century. Later they made and sold shoes, but the shop in this picture is a grocery and general store. Mr Darlison is in the doorway. The date is uncertain, but John Darlison is recorded as being a grocer in Market Street in 1881.

Congreve House, Church Street. The front bay window looked on to the Market Place. The house was home and surgery to the Orton family for nearly a century. Several generations of Ortons were doctors or surgeons in the area.

Dr Edward Orton was born soon after the almshouses were built, and started to practise in 1874 from the house shown opposite. He was a great collector of antiques and was known to have taken items of furniture instead of payment for his medical services. (*Rosemary Hutt–The Orton Collection*)

Dr Orton died in 1904 and his son Lionel took over the practice. It is said that Edward had accumulated so much furniture that Lionel felt obliged to sell some of it at auction. Above are some of the items he sold! (*Rosemary Hutt–The Orton Collection*)

Lionel was a fine figure of a man, generally regarded as the most eligible bachelor in Bedworth, but he did not marry until after the death of both his parents. He then chose a miner's daughter, Margaret, who was twenty-five years his junior. Even now, sixty years after he retired, older people still remember him with great affection. Like his father, he was a collector of coats of armour and old glass. Lionel is shown here in the garden of Congreve House soon after he had qualified, in about 1900. The CD and video counter in Woolworths is now in about the same spot! (*Rosemary Hutt–The Orton Collection*)

Lionel is shown here in one of the cars he enjoyed driving. This one was from about 1918; he is accompanied by his sister. (*Rosemary Hutt–The Orton Collection*)

This is the Orton family's pet monkey, Pongo. A somewhat irascible creature, he once stepped on the hot plate of a cooker that looked cool but wasn't, after which he threw and broke nearly all the crockery in the kitchen. He died after eating soap, a sad if clean end. (*Rosemary Hutt–The Orton Collection*)

Here is the garden of Congreve House with its large pear tree, lawns, greenhouse and Stanley terracotta urn. The site now is the delivery area at the back of Woolworths, a sight too awful to behold. (*Rosemary Hutt–The Orton Collection*)

Inside the greenhouse at Congreve House – a superb picture of Edwardian horticulture. Lionel Orton retired in 1938, but remained active in the town. He helped to run the Home Guard during the war and was a trustee of the almshouses; his wife was a magistrate. However, when the house was required for redevelopment he moved to the south coast where he died in 1964. His wife lived until 1989, but she too was brought back for burial in Bedworth cemetery, and later their daughter, Rosemary, gave all Lionel's written mementoes and pictures to Bedworth library – an act of great thoughtfulness and generosity. Below the buildings that have replaced Church Street and Congreve House, September 2001.

3

Leicester Street

The New Inn stood on the corner of Market Place and Leicester Street. Next but one was the White Swan, later rebuilt. The New Inn was demolished, and there is still a large space at the side of the White Swan. This photograph dates from about 1910. The publican is William Harvey. (*Tony Davis Collection*)

Both the pictures on this page were taken in 1974. The demolition of Leicester Street was under way. The above view was taken from the top of Chapel Street, and was only possible after the Hit or Miss had been demolished because Leicester Street was so narrow. Taylor's music shop is clearly visible. After demolition they moved to All Saints Square, but are now back on the same site in Bede Arcade. The barber's pole is outside the shop used by Gordon Edwards. In 1975 he moved over the road to one of the shops shown on page 40. In 1980 he had to move again to Mill Street. The three-storey building below was Pickering's hat factory. Built in about 1899, the factory was run by George Pickering senior and junior until it closed in 1953.

After hat making finished the factory was taken over by Clear Hooters, as clear an indication as you could find of how important the expanding Coventry motor industry was to outlying towns like Bedworth. This advertisement dates from 1958.

The whole of the west side of Leicester Street, including Bede Arcade is shown above. Tesco covers the old factory site. The hanging baskets were at their best when this was taken in August 2001.

Inside Pickering's hat factory, 1911. The men are making hoods. Flat hoods had sacking inserted to prevent sticking, and then were dipped in shellac for the brim and crown. They were passed through the rollers to remove excess shellac and then through the planking machine to reduce their size.

Where up to 300 were employed making hats, some 19,000 people a week go through the doors at Tesco. I am extremely grateful to Tesco for allowing me to photograph the interior of the store. Here, in September 2001, members of the Tipple family combine shopping with chatting near the cheese display.

After the hoods were shaped into hats they were brought here for trimming. The women in the room at the back trimmed the best quality hats by hand. Off the picture to the right was the machine trimming room. The trimmers added a band and a bow at 3½d a dozen.

The end of the process at Tesco is passing through the elaborate system that reads bar codes, records prices and prints out a bill, all in a split second. No doubt the system also reorders the items you have purchased, and they are replenished within hours. What would Mr Pickering's stock control clerks have made of all that?

Leicester Street, 1948. Just behind the lady was the narrow Old Meeting Yard, which led to the Old Meeting Congregational, now United Reformed, church, a delightful early dissenting chapel dating from 1726. (*Birmingham Central Library*)

Above is the same view in August 2001. The car park on the left is used by a large insurance company in the adjacent large building. They seem to think that scaffolding makes a satisfactory barrier. Perhaps a look at the railings further down the street might inspire them to improve their car park.

The east side of Leicester Street, 1950s. The bus in the distance is one of Payne's, outside the garage now used by Harry Shaw. Beyond that was Hurst's banana warehouse, which was later used as Shoppers Paradise, a precursor of the present KwikSave. (*Ronald Edmands Collection*)

The replacement east side of Leicester Street, August 2001. Neither block has any great architectural merit, though the two gable ends over the office block evoke a memory of similar gables on the old hat factory opposite. The best feature in this photograph is the unique railing designed by Ray Jones and installed, along with the Roanne Garden, as part of the council's millennium celebration.

Samuel Cadman had a bakery and shop
on the corner of Leicester Street and
Chapel Street. In this picture, from about
1904, his wife Emma is in the doorway.
(*Lynda Carnes Collection*)

Shortly after the top picture was taken the bakery was incorporated into the enlarged Hit or Miss,
which is seen on the left-hand corner of this view, dating from the mid-1950s.

THE "HIT OR MISS" INN,

LEICESTER ST., BEDWORTH.

JACK RICHARDS   -   -   Proprietor.

Eadie & Co.'s Fine Burton **Ales & Stout,**

On Draught and in Bottle.

Wines of the Best Quality.   Choice Cigars.

Considerable improvements have recently been effected at this Honse, which is now thoroughly up-to-date, and has every accommodation for Parties, Cyclists, &c.

Jack Richards refers to his recent alterations, which evidently included taking over the Cadman bakery, in this 1907 advertisement that claims that he can now accommodate parties and cyclists.

After the 1974 demolition of The Hit or Miss the new corner shop was taken by florists. There is a long tradition of traders named French in Bedworth. The present owners are not related to them, but have a superb display of flowers in this August 2001 view.

Wyatt's Yard, 1948. Bedworth had many yards, but hardly anyone took photographs of them. This rare view shows the yard that ran through the middle of the large block seen on page 41. The yard ran parallel with Old Meeting Yard. Its name is retained in the sheltered housing behind the office block. (*Birmingham Central Library*)

This 1981 picture shows the space after Wyatt's Yard was demolished. It was taken from the top level of the newly built Tesco store and car park. Within a year or so the new office block was built and the whole landscape changed, but here you can also see the Old Meeting URC on the left, and on the right the building that is now three houses, but was built as a breakaway chapel (Ezra) in the 1840s. It stayed as a chapel for just under 100 years and was the cause of Hob Lane changing its name to Chapel Street. Beyond the car park is the Labour Club that has since been demolished.

An advertising postcard from the 1930s for Thomas Payne's coach firm, then in Newtown Road. Later it moved to Leicester Street, and many people have fond memories of trips on a Payne's coach. The picture below dates from the 1950s and was possibly a Methodist church outing or Sunday school outing. Payne's no longer operates, but the garage is still used by coaches belonging to Harry Shaw.

ARDEN BALLROOM
BEDWORTH

THE LARGEST HALL
in the district — *10,000 square feet of*
PERFECT DANCE FLOOR

MODERN DANCES
at 8 p.m. each
WEDNESDAY & SATURDAY

OLDE TYME BALL
every month
ON FIRST & THIRD THURSDAYS
ON THE REMAINING THURSDAYS
OLDE TYME TUITION

Telephone   3179

YOURS FOR HAPPY DANCING

The Arden Ballroom was immensely popular and many couples met there. Famous dance bands played there; it was unusual for people to have cars, so they looked for entertainment locally. This advertisement dates from 1948.

For over twenty years the Arden Ballroom has been a furniture store, with names varying from Arden Furniture Warehouse, Stuart Edwards, and now Cole's. Generally the only music to be heard is subdued wallpaper music, but in March 2001 Bedworth and Nuneaton hosted a new venture whereby jazz musicians from the City of Birmingham Symphony Orchestra visited six venues in the borough to play jazz and extol the virtues of the CBSO. They are shown here performing for some surprised shoppers in Cole's furniture store, and unconsciously recalling the building's earlier use.

4

Collycroft

Lower Collycroft, as it was called, 1907. The old building jutting into the pavement on the right was pulled down in the 1970s. All the buildings on the left are still here; more were built after 1910 further down the hill. The land beyond is still open, and unless the next local plan goes badly astray, it is likely to remain so, a breathing space between Bedworth and Nuneaton.

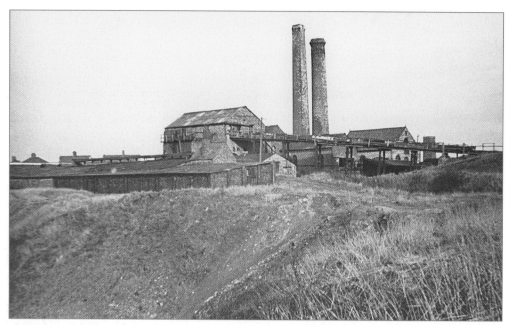

Many Bedworth inhabitants have been employed in the extractive industries over the centuries: coal, clay for brickmaking, ironstone and quarrying, all have contributed to the local economy. This picture shows Blockley's brick works, formerly Downing's, which occupied the land on the corner of Leicester Road and Marston Lane. This area was traditionally the border between Bedworth and Collycroft. There was also a mineral railway line that crossed the main road here from the Charity Colliery, the coal mine that provided most of the income for the 1840 almshouses, and which was about halfway down the present Sutherland Drive. For many years the old clay pits provided water, fun, danger and excitement for local children. As the picture below shows, the area is now an open space with some rather half-hearted rose beds and seats.

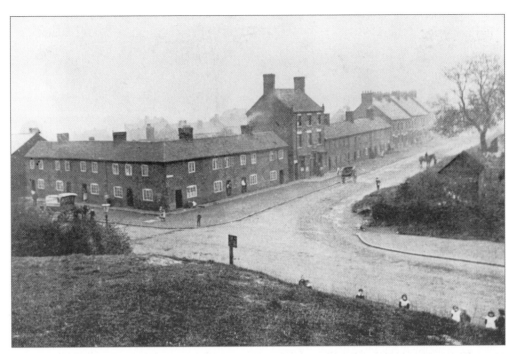

The original cottages on the corner of Marston Lane and the other side of the Miners Arms, 1905.
They were eventually demolished and replaced by the flats seen below. The children in the top
picture are at the bottom of one of the spoil heaps. When Sutherland Drive was built one of the old
pit shafts was uncovered in almost exactly the same spot where the top photograph was taken.

Collycroft School was one of the Chamberlaine charity schools, and it served Collycroft well for a century. One of its pupils was William Johnson, who went on to found the Warwickshire Miners' Association and became Liberal MP for the division from 1906 to 1918. Behind the school, and facing the main road, was the schoolhouse for the headmaster, a building which still exists. One of the most illustrious holders of that post was W.H. Alexander, who went on to become the first headmaster of George Street Council School, the first state school in the town, in 1907. After his retirement he was first chairman of Bedworth Urban District Council. Part of the school wall remains, as can be seen below left. The two houses were built on the school site in Orchard Street.

Old cottages, Nuneaton Road. At the side are the houses up Royal Oak Yard. The degree of subsidence is a bit unnerving, with fence and house leaning in different directions. Robert Evans, father of the writer George Eliot, often inspected poor cottages in Collycroft affected by subsidence on behalf of either Arbury or the Chamberlaine Charity during the 1830s. Even then he used to recommend demolition. The picture above dates from the late 1930s. (*Dorothy Edmands Collection*)

The picture above shows the replacement advertising hoarding in August 2001. I prefer the cottages.

Above is the original Royal Oak, once the scene of a rather macabre murder in the postwar years. (*Ronald Edmands Collection*)

It has since been rebuilt, and, rather oddly, named the Old Royal Oak, shown here in August 2001.

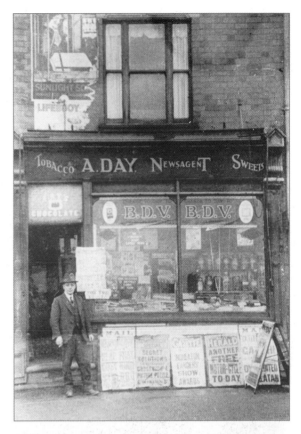

Day's newsagent and sweet shop between the wars, typical of many small businesses in every town, huge numbers of which have been swept away by the spreading tentacles of the supermarkets. The Day family had several shops in Collycroft at various times. Below is the same shop, now with a new front and windows, as the local post office. Day's still have a newsagent and general store on the opposite side of the road from the shops shown here.

The Mann family home in Nuneaton Road, Collycroft, in the early years of the century. Note the lovely wrought iron railings and gate. Latterly, as seen below, the house and its neighbour has been considerably altered and extended to make a residential home for the elderly. The plaque to the left of the door is a Bedworth Society Award for Environmental Excellence. These awards are presented biennially for the restoration of buildings or good new developments. About thirty awards have been made since 1984.

The Cricketers Arms, 1907. The level of the road has risen so that the ground-floor windows seem to be at pavement level, as with many other properties in Collycroft. The three children and a dog make a lovely addition to the picture. The rebuilt pub (below) is attractive, and in the summer it has many visitors who enjoy drinks at the benches outside. Some years ago, when the pub took part in the Borough in Bloom competition, it became one of the most attractive buildings in Collycroft, although it has to be admitted that there was not much competition. The Miners' Arms (page 49) had splendid floral displays in 2001.

Collycroft was home to Daniel Rowbotham's worsted mill and several hundred people were employed there. Rowbotham is buried in a vault near the north door of Bedworth parish church. The factory was converted into housing at the turn of the last century, as shown above. Eventually that was demolished and Catherine Ward Hall residential complex was built on the site. The building below runs at right angles to the line above.

5

Chapel Street

Top of Chapel Street, *c.* 1972. In the distance is the White Swan, which is still here. The rest of the buildings shown have gone. The picture on page 36 was taken about 30 yards up the street from here two years later when demolition had taken place. The present view need not detain us, as it is largely blank wall and the back of the Leicester Street shops. All the buildings shown could have been restored and would by now be highly regarded.

The top of Chapel Street from the Market Place. These views show clearly how this end of Chapel Street has been opened up. The pub on the left has gone, and on the right two buildings, a butcher's and an off-licence, are no more. The railings in the foreground below and in the picture opposite were part of the Millennium Project to renovate this part of Bedworth, and used a design produced and constructed by Ray Jones of Burton Hastings.

Chapel Street, 1948. The little shop has gone and the toilets have been relocated. At the top left is the first-floor bay window of the Hit or Miss (page 58). There seems to have been some peculiarity about Chapel Street or Hob Lane that meant that the houses were built without windows. Another one is seen on page 62. (*Birmingham Central Library*)

The same spot in September 2001 shows Ray Jones's ironwork and Paul Spencer, with his store in the background. Paul is the latest in the family line, starting in 1904, to run a business. More details appear on page 96.

Ezra chapel, early in the twentieth century. The chapel was formed by a dissident group from the Old Meeting, distressed at the Calvinist leanings of their minister, Thomas Dix, a contemporary of Henry Bellairs at the parish church. As in most dissenting chapels, preaching the Word of God was paramount. The tale is told that early in the twentieth century George Pickering Senior (d. 1929) was organist at the Ezra chapel. He also had a hat factory, and during the interminable sermons he would slip off the organ bench and nip up to the factory where he could do half an hour's office work before returning to play for the last hymn! Before the war the chapel closed (the chalice and patten are now in the Parsonage Project Heritage Centre), and the building was converted into the three houses seen below.

Grove Terrace had a very distinctive brick pattern, but now all but one of the houses have been rendered (see opposite, lower picture). All this has happened in the last thirty years. I took the picture above in 1970 before any of the houses were altered. The picture below was taken some ten years earlier and shows Veronica Moore's first class at Hob Lane Infants School. The substantial houses behind Grove Terrace were actually in The Grove. There are a parking space and garages in their place today.

On the extreme left of the top picture was the first large window of Hob Lane Infant School, originally the infant department of the Central School in High Street. Most of the building was demolished and it became a church when the school moved to Furnace Fields. The church, in turn, moved to new premises in Bulkington Road (see page 79). The building is now used as the Julie Bromage Dance Academy. Behind the building (above) is another strangely windowless house. When the area was demolished in the 1950s it was eventually replaced by the flats and bungalows in Cadman Close, named after the bakers already mentioned on page 42.

6

King Street &
Bulkington Road

Coronation celebrations for Edward Vll in 1902. This wonderful view shows the many shops and traders who lived and conducted their business in King Street. Every building has since been demolished.

Had the photographer of the picture on page 63 moved to where the group of children is in the centre of this picture and turned round he would have seen the view above. On the right was the bank (later Midland); the shops are actually in Market Street. The coronation celebrations on page 63 were probably photographed from the top window of Freeman, Hardy & Willis, although they did not actually move there until 1904. The postcard above dates from the end of the First World War.

The same spot in August 2001. Life is sometimes a bit depressing.

Bedworth Sept. 29 1868

Mr & Tools

Bot of J.M. Linney,

Tea Dealer Family Grocer,

CHEESE & BACON FACTOR,

PALMER'S BISCUITS, FOREIGN & BRITISH WINES.

If you turn back to page 63 you will see on the left a low, squat bit of roofline. This was the King's Head (see page 68). The building next to it was J.M. Linney, whose 1861 advertisement is above. For over 200 years the Linney family were important for their contribution to religious (dissenting) and business life in Bedworth. The lovely bill heading shows an engraving of the shop, which remained, although considerably altered, until demolition in the 1970s. (The shop and the one next to it appear on the left of page 71.) (*Owen Buckler Collection*)

J. H. HUSBANDS

HAS A CHOICE SELECTION OF

CHRISTMAS FRUITS

NOTED FOR FIRST-CLASS PROVISIONS.

AGENT FOR . . .

W. & A. Gilbey's Wines & Spirits.

Indian & Ceylon Teas Unsurpassed.

The only address : HUSBANDS, KING STREET, BEDWORTH.

Linney's shop was taken over by J.H. Husbands, whose 1907 advertisement is shown above.

King Street from High Street, *c.* 1965. The old Shoulder of Mutton on the corner, and adjacent shops in King Street had gone, and the fondly remembered Coventry Transport no. 20 bus, with its cream and maroon livery, is leaving for the city. In place now are Nationwide, Lloyds and the *Bedworth Echo* offices in High Street. For the picture below I moved to the corner of King Street to show the buildings that have replaced those seen above across the open space.

Looking down King Street. The shot above was taken in the 1950s, the one below in September 2001. In the 1950s King Street was open to traffic; now it isn't! Below, in the distance on the left, is the ungainly Kings House, which remained empty for its first two years – to the delight of many – and which is now even more unsightly with its plethora of mobile phone masts.

The King's Head was a popular pub, one of the oldest buildings in old King Street. Behind it was a gym that was used by many local boxers for training. The view below shows where the pub used to be, but it includes more adjacent buildings to the left.

This superb postcard view above dates from 1925. On the left is the Old Pheasant Inn, and beyond it is the little road that led into Spitalfields, or Spitaldickey as it was often known. On the right the vehicle is parked outside the King's Head. The old Liberal Club has a balcony outside the first floor (see overleaf). Next to it is a seedsman, but the same shop is shown at an earlier date, on page 72, when it was Austin & Adams, the jewellers. Next to it is the post office, also shown at an earlier date a door or two away, on page 72. (*Geoff Hughes Collection*)

Every building had gone by September 2001.

Bedworth Liberal Club shown during the coronation celebrations for George V, 1911. There was a strong Liberal presence in north Warwickshire, boosted enormously by the presence of William Johnson, founder of the Warwickshire Miners' Association; a man who exemplified the self-help philosophy of Samuel Smiles. He won the parliamentary seat in 1906, defeating the local aristocrat, Francis Newdegate, having defended the seat twice in 1910 against the Conservative candidate, Henry Maddocks. Whether the dog was invited to be in the photograph is not recorded.

Yours faithfully,
W. Johnson.

Printed and Published by Iliffe and Sons Ltd., Vicar Lane, Coventry

Johnson was an extraordinary man, though Lawrence Fretwell recently published (2000) a well-researched counter view to the normal congratulatory comments – many emanating from Johnson himself – and in so doing has shown a much more human figure. The foundation of the Miners' Association was a major achievement. Its fight for rights and pensions, ten years before the state introduced them, was certainly appreciated by miners, who responded long before Johnson was an MP by collecting sufficient funds to build the Miners' Offices and a home for him in 1899. He was the first chairman of the new parish council, and a founder member of the county council.

Between the wars the Liberal Club was rebuilt. It is shown here just before demolition in the early 1970s.

The new 1970s Liberal Club has a huge concert room, but suffers, as do many similar clubs everywhere, from changing fashions in social activities and competition from other aggressive marketing. Also, people's political affiliations have loosened. This picture was taken in August 2001.

Austin & Adams ran this jeweller's shop next to the Liberal Club, although by the time this view was taken, *c.* 1905, J.H. Adams was no longer involved. The shop continued for many years as Austin's elsewhere in town. (*Ted Veasey Collection*)

Bedworth post office, King Street, 1900. In the doorway is the bearded postmaster, Parsons, who had arrived in 1898 and was to remain for thirty years. Holding the horse is Jack Draycott. Behind him are Bill Froggett, and Percy Aucott in the straw hat. Next to Mr Parsons is the young George Jee; his widow lent me the photograph nearly eighty years later. At the time she had just flown back from America at the age of eighty-six!

A quiet day with few people about, King Street, 1948. The shop with the sunblind down was Stubbs, the toyshop and newsagent. It traded in the town for some eighty years until Reg Stubbs junior retired in 2000. (*Birmingham Central Library*)

J.D. Wetherspoon converted the premises, much to the consternation of local publicans and club committees, into a new pub. The buildings this side of Stubbs (in the top picture) were demolished to make way for King's House, the ground floor of which is partly visible on the right of the picture above taken in September 2001.

Botterill & Son were close to Stubbs and in the town for many years. The little leatherware shop below was one of the shops demolished between Edward Road and Bedworth WMC. One wonders whether the dog in front of the Liberal Club on page 70 is the animal that appears here. Was it an itinerant King Street dog with a penchant for photographs, or a pet of the photographer? Could it reach the meat hanging outside Botterill's shop?

Coalpit Fields was one of the earliest settlements around Bedworth; some of the first coal was mined there as early as the seventeenth century. The line of cottages was photographed from the spoil heaps in about 1910 looking towards Woottons and Bulkington Lane in the distance. The spoil heaps have now gone, and a large housing development is being built in its place. Mike and Margaret Lucas, and Jenny and Tony Friel moved into their new houses, not far from the scene above, early in 2001.

Bedworth station, *c.* 1905. There had been some opposition to the proposed railway in 1850, but it was quickly overcome. The station served the town for over a hundred years, bringing in raw materials for the hat factories and beer from Burton-on-Trent. Passengers travelled in huge numbers to Coventry during the early twentieth century, and the train timetable was published in the parish magazine.

During the early 1900s the old wooden station buildings were replaced with brick ones, and later a canopy was added. This view, looking towards Bulkington Road, shows the station as many will remember it. On the left is Railway Terrace. The picture was taken in 1965 when the station was closed under the sweeping changes brought about by Dr Beeching. (*Geoff Edmands Collection*)

Cartage teams preparing to leave Bedworth station, at that time – the 1920s – part of the LNWR.
No doubt they were delivering barrels of beer to the many local pubs.

Fortunately Dr Beeching's axe did not lead to the removal of the line, as it was used spasmodically
for freight. In the 1980s the station platform was rebuilt, along with a shelter. The picture shows it
on the official reopening day in 1988 when railway buffs came from far and wide to celebrate. Very
few people use the service now, which is sad because it takes you to and from Coventry very quickly.

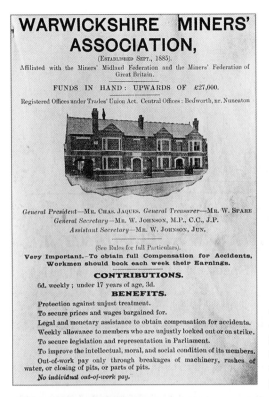

An advertisement for Warwickshire Miners' Association, 1907. William Johnson, as general secretary, was a key worker for the association, which raised the issues of safety, compensation and pensions long before they gained national importance.

This splendid photograph shows a group of men who look pretty pleased with themselves, as well they might. They are celebrating the opening of the Miners' Offices in Bulkington Road. On their lapels they are all wearing a woven bookmark, of the type still produced by Cash's, which includes pictures of the offices and Johnson. One of these special locally woven bookmarks is on display in The Parsonage Project (see page 128).

Miners' Welfare Offices, 1987. Coalmining declined rapidly in the 1980s and entire communities ceased to have a purpose or an income. There were repercussions even in towns like Bedworth that had more of a mixed economy. The old Miners' Welfare Offices, so worthy in their prime, and so worthy of a place in the town's history, were partly demolished by permission of a council that showed a distressing lack of awareness of the building's symbolic as well as real importance. Below is the rump of the building in September 2001, with some inelegant alterations. The offices were partially demolished to give access to the new Christian Centre. The church is built on the site of the old gas works.

Some of the workers from Wootton's hat factory in the early 1900s. The picture below shows the rear of the factory that had originally been Paddy Hart's, and which suffered dreadfully when the ribbon-weaving industry collapsed in 1860. The whole rambling collection of factory and workshop buildings has been tumbling down for at least thirty years. As this book goes to press the buildings are finally disappearing, the land is being cleared and roads are being laid. Houses will eventually be built on the site.

The derelict factory, 1970. Other users of factory space had been Coventry Hood and Sidescreen, a name wonderfully redolent of the early motor industry in nearby Coventry. The large factory disappeared, but the picture below, taken in September 2001, shows part of the old wall converted into another factory unit, now also derelict. By the time this book is published the entire site will have been cleared.

Navigation Row, early 1900s. The Navigation Inn (not shown here) is the only clue as to the whereabouts of this line of terraced houses. It was part of a little community that grew up around the bridge over the Coventry Canal, and stood to the east of the pub. The present-day Columbia Gardens, seen below in August 2001, are somewhere near the original Navigation Row.

7

High Street

Taken from High Street, 1948. The photographer was standing outside what is now Lloyds Bank and was looking back towards Market Street and Market Place. Warrington's was on the corner of King Street (see page 67). The picture overleaf was taken from about the same distance, but from the other side of the road. (*Birmingham Central Library*)

High Street, looking towards Market Street and King Street, mid-1950s. The Shoulder of Mutton was the pub on the corner. The half-timbered, mock-Tudor, actually late 1890s, building was the Midland Bank. After redevelopment the Midland (now HSBC) moved to its present position at the top of All Saints Square (just visible on page 29). During the early 1970s the old Midland building was used as a temporary post office while the old one was rebuilt. Some twenty years later the post office moved again to the Co-op (see page 91). Below is the same spot in August 2001.

High Street, 1950s. The Co-op was in Bedworth from the early 1900s. Their shop was rebuilt in 1929 and has a pleasing aspect, now sustained largely by the presence of the post office. Just beyond the Co-op part of a tree can be seen. This was a large pear tree in the front garden of the Tower House (see page 91). In the distance are two pubs side by side, the Beehive and the Haunch of Venison. On the extreme right the dark section of building is the Girls' Central School. (*Ronald Edmands Collection*)

Not quite the same angle but from very near the same spot as the picture above. This shows the staff of the *Bedworth Echo*, which has reported on life, or some of it, in Bedworth since 1979. Pictured are Matt Barron, John Harris, Lesley Harrison, Mary Rose, editor Mort Birch, Jane Stirland, and Penny Cryer. The paper was started by two local reporters, Mort Birch and Alan Robinson, who ran it for about fifteen years before it became part of the Trinity Mirror Group.

The old parish church, *c.* 1880. The oldest part of All Saints' parish church is the tower, which might be fifteenth century. During the nineteenth century the church went from almost disastrous negligence by the Hon. Mr Finch, who came as rector in 1816 and promptly left for France, to Henry Bellairs who extended the building twice during his forty-five year incumbency. Later Frederic Evans launched an enthusiastic rebuilding scheme which succeeded and produced the present building in 1890. The picture above shows the east end and chancel from High Street. With its wide side aisles it was almost square inside, with a balcony reminiscent of a nonconformist chapel. Below is the tower and west end of the old church in about 1880.

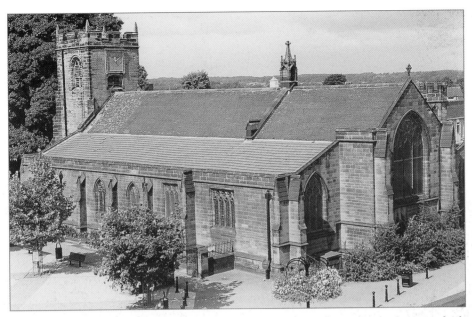

The 1890 church is a splendid example of late Victorian gothic by Bodley and Garner, built of Runcorn stone by Thompson and Son of Peterborough. The north side was opened up by the development of All Saints Square, and in recent years the south side has come into its own with the development of the Health Centre and open quadrangle on the old central school site (see page 92). This view was taken in September 2001 from the roof of the Civic Hall.

This interior view of the church dates from the 1930s. When the church was first opened there was no rood screen. One was provided in memory of Mr Wootton, and it remained in position until 2000.

New interior, parish church, 2000. The Church decided it needed radical thinking to face the challenge of twenty-first century ministry. The old 1950s parish hall was sold and a new inner building, or narthex, was constructed at the west end of the church to provide meeting rooms, offices, toilets, kitchen and social space. The rood screen was moved from its traditional place across the chancel and raised on to the wall of the narthex, as this picture shows. Architect David Slade transformed the building. It is now carpeted and welcoming, and can be visited most days. The scheme won an Outstanding Environmental Improvement Award and plaque from the Bedworth Society in 2001. (*Colin Finch*, Bedworth Echo)

It is extraordinary, with the perfect vision afforded by hindsight, how casually we throw away buildings of quality. The picture of All Saints Row above shows a line of interesting buildings, well proportioned and visually attractive, with pitched roofs, where people could live close to the town centre. (*Ken Bosworth Collection*)

Above is its replacement, the Midland, now HSBC, in August 2001. Enough said. Daniel Rowbotham (see page 56) is buried in the table vault in the middle of the picture.

The High Street, *c.* 1905. It shows a High Street that was always wider than the other main streets in town. On the right are the church and the old Girls' Central School (the apparent church window was the hall of the school).

In August 2001 everything, apart from the church, has gone. All is not lost however, as some of the redeveloped High Street is extremely good.

The Tower House, High Street, 1930s. During the early nineteenth century the house was owned by the Linneys. It was then bought by the Edmands family who ran a number of ribbon-related industries, latterly frilling and electric lampshade trimmings. The tower had been built by an early enthusiastic amateur astronomer, but during the war it was used for one of the air raid sirens. The front garden, so close to the town centre, was delightful. (*Ronald Edmands Collection*)

The Tower House and adjacent buildings were demolished in 1963 and the extension to the Co-op built on the site. The Co-op now specialises in travel, holiday sales and electrical goods, as well as housing the post office and a hairdresser. It is also a funeral directors. All this is a far cry from the days when the Co-op was a major grocer in the town.

The view after the Tower House was demolished in 1963. Ronald Edmands stands on the site of his family home. Across the road is the Girls' Central School. Ronald is standing where people now queue in the post office. (*Geoff Edmands Collection*)

The picture above was taken in August 2001 from where the JCB is in the picture above. It shows the excellent Health Centre, built in the playground of the old Central Schools, and the open space that allows such a good view of the church. The modern 1990s and gothic 1890s buildings co-exist quite happily. From 1715 until 1840 the almshouses were on the site.

Spitalfields, or Spitaldickey's was a warren of poor, cramped housing and ribbon weavers' dwellings that lay behind High Street, bounded on the east by Rye Piece (which originally only went from King Street to the Miners' Welfare Park) and on the south by the Zion Baptist chapel and the park. It was probably so called because it was on land opposite the first almshouses, or hospital (a word which has changed its meaning considerably since 1715; indeed the correct name is still the Nicholas Chamberlaine Hospital and Sermon Charity). This view was taken from the top of Tower House in 1948. (*Birmingham Central Library*)

The same view from the Civic Hall roof in September 2001. The whole site was cleared during the late 1960s, the last bit to go being the lovely Zion chapel, built in 1798, and visible in the top picture. It stood just by the present entrance to the Civic Hall car park. The splendid new chapel, by Keith Corrigan, is in Newdegate Road.

High Street, 1950s. Some of the larger buildings were quite elegant, and the Haunch of Venison had been a coaching inn in earlier years. Next to it was the Beehive, and closer was the Silver Key Photographic Studies, which had moved from Sleath's Yard. (*Ronald Edmands Collection*)

This is the building which replaced them, the Civic Hall, bequeathed by the UDC before it was forced by Ted Heath's government into a shotgun marriage with Nuneaton in 1974. The City of Birmingham Symphony Orchestra plays here regularly, as does Ken Dodd. It is now widening its appeal, out of necessity, to compete with Warwick Arts Centre and the cosmopolitan choice of events in Birmingham. Of all the new (i.e. post-1965) buildings in the town, the Civic Hall is one of the best. Most of the other good buildings are also in High Street.

Above: High Street, *c.* 1914; below: September 2001. Every building from above has gone, though the Co-op is on the same site. The shop behind the group of onlookers above was occupied by J. Spencer and Son (see page 96). Before they moved there it had been used by Mr Dewis as a pawn shop. On Empire Day 1910 a monkey set fire to the shop by knocking over a lamp on the top floor. Children from the central school were on their way to one of the fields where the park now is, and watched as the firemen tried to tackle the flames. The fire station was only a few yards away, adjacent to the old council offices (see page 100).

John Spencer, with his sons Fred and Walter, outside the shop in High Street, *c.* 1920. The distinctive enamel letters on the windows were a common form of advertising. Often they would drop off and leave gaps. Even after their removal they often left a shadow of the original letter on the glass. That happened with this window, part of which was rescued when demolition took place, and it is still in the garage of a member of the Bedworth Society. (*Jean Thompson Collection*)

Spencer's eventually left High Street and moved to the top of Newtown Road, before moving to their present site in Chapel Street (see page 59). The shop was taken over by G. & F. Evans; this is of one of their payment cards from 1932.

There had been a lending library in Chapel Street as early as 1851. The County Library later ran a service in the Johnson Memorial Pavilion in the Miners' Welfare Park. It then moved to part of the old Dewis brewery in Rye Piece. In 1955 it moved to the building on the right (see pages 95 and 96). As expectations rose there was pressure for about twenty years for a new purpose-built library. This was eventually provided on land adjacent to the site shown here in the late 1980s, and the old library site was redeveloped as the council's Bedworth Area Office, linked to the Civic Hall. It is shown (below) in September 2001.

There were two White Lion pubs. The other one was in a yard off the Market Place. The top picture shows the pub in the High Street in about 1912 before it was given a new front. In the door stand Ethel and Helena Cleaver (her married name was Bolstridge), whose family kept the pub for many years. (*Ann Crutchlow Collection*)

The White Lion was a significant building as one approached High Street from Coventry Road, seen below in 1988. At its side were the gates and pathway alongside some cottages leading to the Zion Baptist chapel. The Coventry tram (introduced in 1880) started from here, and the area was popularly known as the 'Top o' the trams'. The tram service ceased in 1940 (see cover).

High Street, 1950s. On the right is more evidence of the original ribbon-weaving top shops, probably late eighteenth century, with narrower windows than the later nineteenth-century top shops in Mill Street (see page 105). On the left can be seen the old Bedworth UDC offices and the old Central School beyond. On this side of the council offices was the fire station, and below is the fire engine that was housed there in the 1920s.

The picture above shows the Bedworth Council Offices, dating from 1900, and the headmaster's house for the Central School, built in 1880, but later used as council offices. There was much local opposition to their demolition, spearheaded by the Bedworth Society in 1982 and 1983, but the decision to build the new police headquarters was taken and the building shown below was constructed. It is a fine building, using brick in interesting ways, recalling the brick-making tradition in the area. Despite opposing the development the Bedworth Society recognised the quality of the replacement and gave it a plaque for environmental excellence. Unfortunately it has never been displayed on the building because Warwickshire Constabulary lost it. There is a moral there somewhere.

8

Water Tower, Park Road & Mill Street

The view from the water tower, looking over Ambleside Road, 1988. By then the tower was no longer in use. The site was sold, houses erected and the tower, 150 ft high and a listed building, remains for a developer with enough cash to convert it to splendid apartments.

For over sixty years the water tower stood alone on the edge of the town, but the picture above shows the footings of the estate that now encloses the east and south sides, roads like Briardene Avenue and Gibson Crescent, which were built in the 1960s and are seen below. The tower can be seen for many miles. In 1910 Alison Evans, daughter of Canon Evans, the rector, wrote in her journal as she was returning from a holiday: 'When I saw the water tower, I could hardly keep up a demure appearance before the passengers.'

Above is Faulconbridge's Bakery delivery horse and cart pausing in Park Road (originally Roadway) in the 1950s. Faulconbridge was one of several bakers in the town. His store was in King Street, and he was one of many businessmen and traders who contributed to the political, religious or social life of the town. The building behind the horse was the Anchor pub, which was demolished in 2000. (*Ronald Edmands Collection*)

The site behind the bakery was developed in the early 1970s as a supermarket (though advertised as the country's first hypermarket). It is a utilitarian building, which for a time caught the imagination of local people, because it was the creation of two local businessmen who had used the old banana warehouse in Leicester Street to offer bargain prices and bulk quantities at a time when the abolition of retail price maintenance was a gleam in Ted Heath's eye. It was a matter of pride to Bedworth that people flocked from Coventry to buy cheap alcohol. The success of this venture, called Shoppers Paradise, led to the purpose-built store above, which is now suffering genteel decline in the hands of Somerfield/Kwik Save.

Fronting Mill Street, where the market and KwikSave are, stood some nineteenth-century ribbon weaving houses and top shops. Behind them Thomas Peake built his house in the 1860s. He had an interest in the Mill Street properties, and his ribbon-weaving factory later moved further down Newtown Road. Above is Brooke Peake in his car, parked in front of Mill House in the 1920s. Below is KwikSave in September 2001; the store was built on part of Peake's land. It makes a striking contrast.

Mill Street, 1948. There were several substantial buildings. The shop on the left-hand corner was a baker and confectioner; the old bill headings shown on pages 10 and 65 came from that building, where they were bricked into a range in about 1902. The bills to Mrs Lovell date from the 1860s, but bricked in with them was a bottle of unopened beer brewed for the coronation of Edward Vll. (*Birmingham Central Library*)

The same part of Bedworth spoilt by the continuing presence of through traffic in August 2001.

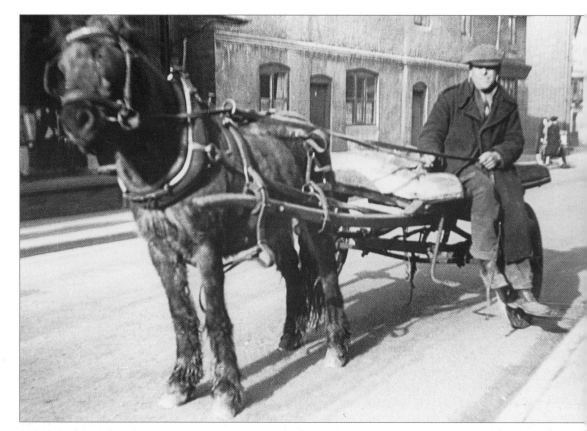

Delivery cart and elderly horse, Mill Street, 1950s. The shop behind the horse's head was pulled down and redeveloped – Tesco's first shop in Bedworth was there. In 1980 they moved to their present store, and Iceland now occupies the site. (*Ronald Edmands Collection*)

The other buildings, much altered but probably eighteenth century in origin, are still there as Harry and Rose's bakery.

9

School

Children from the Catholic School, Bedworth, Friday 29 May 1908. Oh, that all photographs were as accurately recorded. Catholicism returned to Bedworth in 1875 when a group of Catholics met in Sleath's Yard, and later in Leicester Street. A small church and school were opened in Rye Piece in 1883. It had an impact on the Central Schools, and the log book records that several girls were sent to the Catholic School because it cost less. In 1894 a new school was built for 200 pupils and the church was enlarged. It is this school that the children above attended. They look quite a happy group compared with some pictures from the same era.

George Street School, 1986, taken from the top car park of Tesco. This superb building was replicated all over the country during the early years of the twentieth century, following the 1902 Education Bill, which finally put paid to school boards and established local education authorities with wide-ranging responsibilities.

Sadly, there seemed little support at county council level for any scheme to retain the building for community and/or commercial use, and eventually the site became a petrol station and car park, as shown above in September 2001. A wonderful opportunity was lost, and with it a fine 1907 building. The first head of the school was W.H. Alexander, a man of great talent, and later to be first chairman of Bedworth UDC.

Nicholas Chamberlaine Comprehensive School has no connection with the charity that supports the four primary Church of England schools in Bedworth, but there is a historical link. Following the 1944 Education Act authorities had to establish separate primary and secondary schools, so the days of the all-age school were numbered. The Chamberlaine School trustees decided to concentrate on primary schools, but the new comprehensive was built on land once owned by the charity. The new school opened in 1955; the rather formal PE display by girls at the opening is shown above. The picture below shows the much less formal final day of compulsory education for these year 11 girls in June 2001. They dressed up specially and were joined for this photograph by their young-looking year head, Mary Somerville (on the right). (*Colin Finch*, Bedworth Echo)

The Revd Henry Bellairs, in 1857, possibly the most important cleric in nineteenth-century Bedworth. He came as curate in 1819, later became rector, transformed the church, enlarging it twice, and became the scourge of immorality and scurrilous behaviour in the town, before retiring in 1864. He had fought at Trafalgar as a very young sailor (he was born in 1790), was wounded, joined the army, married into a wealthy family and then joined the church. During his time here the almshouses were rebuilt and the Central Schools built. He brought life to the slumbering charity so that it had a major impact on the life and prosperity of Bedworth, a task continued in 1876 by the Revd F.R. Evans. Bellairs had thirteen children, one of whom died at birth. One became a chief inspector of schools, another was curate of Bedworth for many years, and daughter Nona donated about a quarter of the costs for rebuilding the church in 1890.

When Collycroft School closed a new school was built at Furnace Fields and named after Henry Bellairs. The tradition of remembering important citizens in this way is highly commendable (e.g. Canon Evans and Canon Maggs). How sad then that Henry Bellairs, the greatest of them all, has now been lost; the school merged with the local infants' school and was renamed after St Michael. There is nothing wrong with calling a school after a saint, but St Michael is already patron saint of Coventry and has a statue by Jacob Epstein (on the outside wall of St Michael's Cathedral) in his honour. It would have been much better to have retained the name of one of Bedworth's genuine church militants. The picture shows departing headmaster Andrew Gilroy with some of his pupils on the last day of term in July 2001.

Boys' Central School, *c.* 1925. The class was Standard 5B and the teacher was Mr Johnson. He owned a Matchless motorcycle and the top boy had the honour of cleaning it! Arthur Neale is on the extreme right of the picture. Later he was A.H. Lawrence's head monitor. This meant clerk, office boy, errand boy and general factotum. But Arthur enjoyed the job, because he was able to wander anywhere on the school premises and around the town carrying out the headmaster's instructions.

When the central schools closed a new school opened in Derwent Road named after Canon Maggs. The pupils shown in this picture were members of a gardening club. In 2000 the school won the 'Best School in the Borough' award for its floral efforts. Shown here with some of their 2001 displays are Andrew Sear, Ryan Thomas, Rebecca Harrison, Alison Mawn, Rachel Squires, Brandon Grace, Laura Heritage, Natalie Stein, Esther Dudfield, Isaac Al-Hindawi, Samuel King, Gary Holden and Emmi Burton. Miss Grisedale is the teacher.

Bedworth Evening Continuation Gardening Class with their instructor Mr T.P. Harrison, 1905. Bedworth had many evening classes at this time, catering for those who had only acquired a brief education but wanted to learn more. Standing, left to right: A. Ison, T. Marsden, S. Bosworth, H. Dodd, C. Cole, E. Taylor, H. Neale, H. Marsden, E. Neale, J. Neale. Seated: F. Shortridge and R. Cooper.

St Giles Junior School, Exhall. These pupils, under the inspired guidance of Jane Stokes, swept all the awards at the 2001 Britain in Bloom schools' sections, taking three major prizes. The pupils here, all year six, were photographed in July 2001 standing by one of the gardens created in the school. This one shows a wartime garden with an air raid shelter used as a garden shed. From left to right the pupils are Paul McKinzie, Hartej Hayer, Pardeep Sandhu, Shane Whetstone, Cheryl Hurn and Sherry Broadhurst.

10

Work

Coventry Colliery at Keresley before closure. The colliery employed hundreds of men; many of them came from Scotland and the north-east during the 1950s to help work this profitable pit. Later the smokeless fuel plant was added. The 1984 strikes saw men striving to retain their livelihoods and a sense of purpose for Keresley. The battle was lost, but the new Prologis Park is bringing some jobs and more economic hope to the area. Before long a generation will see the new units and distribution warehouses and be unaware of the toil that was once a feature of this coal-mining community.

The 1830s saw the opening of what was to be known as the Charity Colliery at Collycroft. It was profitable and produced the income that was to fund the rebuilding of the almshouses, and the enormous expansion of schools. This picture from the early twentieth century shows the men employed in the carpenters' shop at the colliery. The mine closed in 1926, but there was a brick works on the site for several more decades. The housing estate running off Sutherland Drive now occupies the colliery site.

We have already seen pictures of the Magson shop in Market Place (page 17). Another arm of the business was in the building trade in the 1920s. Here employees of the firm are posing for the camera before a day's work.

The Coventry Canal at Bedworth Hill. The pub shown here was always known as Shaw's, after the family who ran it. This is close to bridge thirteen, near Coalpit Fields, and there was an arm, out of which the barge is emerging, that allowed coal to be brought from the Newdigate Colliery by rail and then transferred to the canal. (*Ronald Edmands Collection*)

In September 2001 the pub had gone, and so had the little community that grew up round it on the ground behind the boat above. The canal is now used extensively during the summer months by tourists and canal enthusiasts who can cope with never going at more than 4 miles an hour.

The Newdigate Colliery was sunk in 1898 and closed in February 1982. The picture above was taken during the last week of work. The pit provided work for several generations of Bedworth men, and the Woodlands area was criss-crossed with footpaths leading to and from the mine. The winding wheel from the shaft was retained and installed a few years later in the Miners' Welfare Park, an apt and excellent decision by the local council. Now houses are built where the shower block used to stand, and all trace of an industry that employed hundreds has disappeared.

Exhall Colliery, *c.* 1930. The colliery site was an extensive one and included, at its northern end, the Exhall Brick and Tile Co., many of whose derelict buildings lingered on until the 1980s for storage, motor repairs and so on. Today the Bayton Road Industrial Estate occupies the site of the colliery and brickworks. On the whole it is untidy, litter-strewn and the result of earlier haphazard planning. As one drives through it to the northern end that was developed later, there is some improvement in the appearance, but the overwhelming impression is depressing.

As coal use declined oil and gas took over. There is a certain irony that on part of the old Exhall Colliery site there is now the Murco Oil depot, seen here in September 2001.

This piece of wall is the only remaining fragment of the old colliery and brickworks fragment, September 2001. It was one of the brickyard buildings with those typical rounded windows and metal frames that made so many nineteenth-century factories look like chapels.

The northern end of Bayton Road Industrial Estate, September 2001. These newer buildings are good of their type. The link with the past comes from the fact that they are on Colliery Lane.

11

Celebration

The winning team, September 2001. Nuneaton & Bedworth Borough Council has entered the annual Britain in Bloom competition fourteen times, and has won numerous awards. The borough now has an enviable reputation throughout the Midlands for its floral displays. A key feature every year is the Miners' Welfare Park in Bedworth. In 1923 the Miners' Welfare Committee handed over the land it had purchased in 1921 to the parish council, and the park has been nurtured, expanded and loved ever since. In 2000 it was given an award as 'Best Park in Britain' by the national Britain in Bloom judges, and in 2001 it again contributed to the borough's success in winning the Heart of England regional award. The men and women in the photograph were those whose hard work and dedication make the borough so attractive throughout the year. The Wedgwood cup in the picture will be retained for a year.

The First World War had a devastating effect on our communities, and all over the country memorials were built. Bedworth lost 207 men of the 1,200 who enlisted; their memorial was unveiled in 1921, as shown above. After the Second World War more names were added. Gradually the original idea of holding a memorial service at 11 a.m. on 11 November ceased, in favour of an Armistice Day service on the nearest Sunday. However, in Bedworth a small group of men insisted on maintaining the original service, and so Bedworth is now the only place where the tradition has been unbroken.

In the last twenty years Bedworth's Armistice Day efforts have grown in scope so that the town is full of ex-servicemen and women, and media coverage is extensive. This picture was taken during the 1998 parade, one which had a particular poignancy eighty years after the end of the First World War.

The picture above reputedly shows the first bicycle in Bedworth with pneumatic tyres. The owner seems proud of his bike, despite having no mudguards, gears or lamps. Below a lad is enjoying the exhilarating experience of taking off on his bike at the new skate park in Bedworth, which, since it opened in April 2001, has allowed youngsters to ride and skate without endangering the public in the town centre – though some of them still do that.

Bedworth United, 1926. There has been a long tradition of soccer in Bedworth, and in earlier years teams were fielded by pubs, clubs, churches and factories – wherever men gathered together and could make a team. The Bedworth United team goes back for about a century.

The Bedworth United squad for 2001–2. They play at the Oval before a dedicated crowd of a few hundred supporters, which can swell to a few thousand when they play rivals Nuneaton Borough. Back row, left to right: Scott Brown, Indepaul Khela, Jamie Smith, Craig Glover, Danny Smith, Pat Patterson (goalkeeping coach), Tynan Scope, Karl Phillips, Adam Kinder, James Richardson. Middle row: Marcus Law (assistant manager), Adam Webster, Paul Rostron, Spencer Parsons, Nathan Thompson, Paul John, Matt Abbicrombi, Scott McGregor, Pete Heggarty, Amrit Sidhu, John Husselby, Andy Harty, Ian Croston (reserve team manager). Front row: Martin Crowley, Andy Morson, Paul White, Guy Sanders (club captain), Pete Randle (chairman), Ian Drewitt (player/manager), Mark Robinson (team captain), Craig Whitmore, Ashley Pringle, Robert Oddy. (*Matt Barron, Bedworth Echo*)

This is the earliest picture of Bedworth Cricket Club, and it shows the victorious team as winners of the 1907 Coventry & District League Cup. Back row, left to right: -?-, J. Spencer, J. Waterfall, H. Bonsor, Mr Simpson, H. Simpson. Middle row: Mr Aubrey (umpire), C. Taberer, J. Shaw, E. Darlison, J. Wale, P. Broadfoot, Mr Watts (umpire). Seated: Canon F.R. Evans (Rector and Oxford cricket blue 1864–6), W. Hall, A. Wyatt, P. Scutt, H. Earl, J. Gallagher, Mr Carter. On the ground: A. Randle, F. Bosworth.

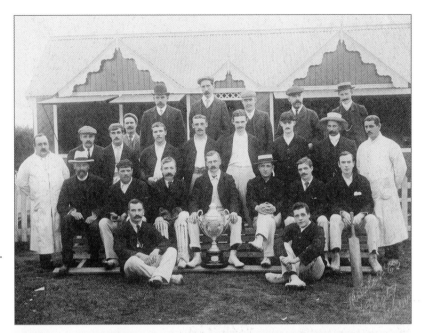

Bedworth Cricket Club, August Bank Holiday Monday, 2001. Back row, left to right: Hussein Caratella, Dennis Oakes, Tom Brindley (president), Craig Friswell, Paul Cronin, Paul Haynes. Front row: Vickesh Patel, Doug Marillier, Mark Spacey, Richard Iles, Omar Choudhry. During the 2001 season Doug Marillier played test cricket for Zimbabwe.

The Old Meeting United Reformed church, or the Old Meeting, has a long history and has made a remarkable contribution to life in Bedworth. Founded by Julius Saunders in 1686, a prominent dissenter who had served a prison sentence at Warwick for his beliefs, the church community met in Bedworth to escape the effect of the Five Mile Act after the Restoration, and built the church in 1726. This picture dates from about 1910 and shows the Ladies Bible class. (*Marion Case Collection*)

Old Meeting Sunday school anniversary, April 2001. The whole congregation cooperated by lining up in the same place as the young ladies above. In the top picture the minister was the Revd F. Bradley (1908–22). Below and in the same position on the right is the minister, the Revd Leslie Giller.

Whit Walks, Sunday school anniversaries, church anniversaries, carnivals, coronations: all were cause for celebration and often for walking or marching around town. Many of them started, finished or both at the almshouses, and there are countless pictures of such events in the quadrangle there. This picture, probably from the 1950s, shows girls from Mill Street Methodist church being presented with their prize certificate in the Bedworth Carnival Parade. Among the dignitaries is MP Frank Bowles. (*Kate Richardson Collection*)

Between the wars hundreds would take part in the Whit Walk when members of most of the churches in town walked round the town witnessing their faith. Gradually numbers declined until it was decided to abandon the walk. In very recent years, however, several churches wanted to restore some of the old community spirit and witness, and they decided to have a picnic and service in the park on Whit Sunday. 2001 saw the event take place in good weather in June, and four children are shown here participating with their flags. They are Hannah Beck, Clare Rogers, Lauren Owen and Dayle Stanley.

Founder's Day, Bedworth Almshouses. The Revd Nicholas Chamberlaine instructed his trustees to build almshouses and schools when he died in 1715. He also instructed them to ensure that during Whit week every year a sermon should be preached for which the preacher would be paid 10s. During the early nineteenth century the residents, or inmates, were given a meal and replacement uniform on Founder's Day, or Bun Day as it became known after 1864, when the children from all the church schools were given a currant bun instead of the meal they formerly had. This delightful picture shows a very respectful little girl graciously accepting her bun, probably during the 1940s or 1950s. The picture below shows Bun Day on 25 May 2001. This was the last time the banners of Hob Lane and Henry Bellairs Schools appeared in public, as they have now become St Michael's Primary School. Beneath the balloons are the mayor and mayoress, Cllrs Bill and Sheila Hancox.

For photographers Bun Day is a dream! For the children, one hopes it is something they remember, so long as they learn why it is all happening and who they are honouring. In earlier years the governors would give the children a half holiday on Bun Day, but since the throttling effect of league tables and Ofsted the practice has ceased. These children are singing the much loved 'The School of our Church'.

When he is an old man Alex Macdonald will be able to boast to his grand-children that he had a bun when he was only one year old, and that he has a picture to prove it! Large numbers of buns are baked for the 1,100 or so pupils, but sometimes they go to other mouths. We can excuse Alex since he provides such a lovely picture.

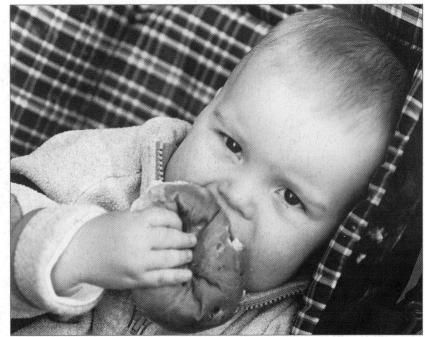

The Parsonage Project is a heritage centre in the cellar of one of the Nicholas Chamberlaine Almshouse buildings. It is run by the Bedworth Society, a civic amenity society founded in 1981. Part of the centre tells the story of Chamberlaine and his impact on the town. The picture above shows the first birthday cake for the project on 4 February 2001, exactly 337 years since Chamberlaine came to Bedworth as rector. Our mannequin is flanked by Ada and Abe, the models of residents in their uniform from 1910, made for the centre by Jo Bannister.

The Parsonage Project has a similar purpose to this book – illuminating the present by understanding the past, and it is striking chords with Bedworth residents. The picture shows some of the supporters, committee and stewards of the heritage centre. Back row, left to right: Bill White, Abe, Ralph Mounter, Joyce Taylor, Vince Taylor, Pat Lawlor, John Lawlor, Tony Baylis, Doug Leighton, Lynda Carnes. Front row: Marion Baylis, Molly Davies, Edna Leighton, Jean White, Joan McKenna, Kath Riley.